Published by
FORMING LIVES INC

Copyright © 2020 by
GOOD WORD TRUST

Title
MY BEST ME - Textbook 3

Editor-In-Chief
Josien Knigge

Authors
Amy Nevares
Elizabeth Palmer Solon
Anne Marie Wahls
Josien Knigge

Editor
Virdeen J. Muñoz

Revision and Correction
Josien Knigge

Technical Editor
Carlos A. Ferrufino

Cover Design
Ziza Zoe Malloy

Special thanks to Dr. Chan Hellman and
the OU-Tulsa Hope Research Center
for their curriculum content review.

HOPE RESEARCH CENTER
The UNIVERSITY of OKLAHOMA - TULSA

ISBN-13: 978-1-951061-21-0

Hope Rising SEL
PO Box 722255
Norman, OK 73070
United States
Tel: (405) 676-4140
Mail: info@hoperisingsel.com
www.hoperisingsel.com

4.0.7. usa

HOPE

Who do you want to be? What do you want to do when you grow up? ... be an athlete? ... own a business? ... travel the world? ... be an inventor? Do you see yourself happy and secure?

The science and power of hope gives you the ability to make tomorrow better than today. Anything that you want to be, to do or to have will happen because of hope? Hope turns regular individuals into superstars. Hope gives soldiers, sailors, airmen and marines courage and valor to win impossible battles. Hope turns everyday people into heroes who are able to conquer fear and adversity.

My Best Me will train you to have hope. Your hope will increase as you learn about emotions and how to manage them. You will discover the value of relationships in building a better tomorrow. More hope means better grades, thoughts, emotions, and behavior. Hope is a better future. *My Best Me* will teach you that hope is not a wish or an emotion; it is a personal decision. Anybody can have hope no matter who you are or the challenges you face.

Think of Hope as being a treasure map.

1. **Set a goal:** Your goal is the treasure: the things you want to be, and do and have. What are your dreams and visions? They can help set your goals.
2. **Find a path:** Your path is the route to the treasure; the steps and plans you need to make and take to reach your goals.
3. **Build up willpower:** Your willpower is the desire and strength to get to your goals; if your goals are important to you, nothing will stop you.

Going Deeper

1. **Set Goals** – This is finding out WHAT you want to be, do or have and WHEN you want to be, do or have it.

   a. Setting a goal only works if it is something you really want.
   b. A goal should be very specific and simple.
   c. The goal can be something you want to be, do or have soon. That is called a short term goal.
   d. The goal can be something you want to be, do or have in the future. That is called a long term goal.
   e. A goal with a date is more powerful because a goal without a date is a dream.
   f. Write down every goal you have and put those goals where you can see them often.
   g. Define in detail what your goal means to you

2. **Find Pathways** – This is finding out HOW you will achieve your goal. Which steps will you need to take on the route to your goal.

   a. A pathway always starts where you are and leads to your goal.
   b. A pathway is a series of small steps that you take in the direction of your goal.
   c. More than one path can lead to your goal.
   d. Very few paths lead straight to your goal, they twist and turn.
   e. The path can change many times on the way to your goal.

3. **Build up Willpower** – This is finding out WHY you will achieve your goals. If your goals are truly important to you, you will have what it takes to succeed.

   a. Willpower is an inner strength and desire you need to reach your goal
   b. Willpower is found inside of you.
   c. Willpower will produce the energy you need to succeed.
   d. The greatest goals in the world and best pathways are nothing unless there is willpower to succeed.

"My Best Me" is your guide to discovering your true identity and purpose. Hope is important for your journey. Knowing who you are is the same as knowing where you are. When choosing goals and deciding on a pathway, knowing where you are gives you a place to start! Having a place to start will give you great confidence, a good attitude and the willpower to succeed.

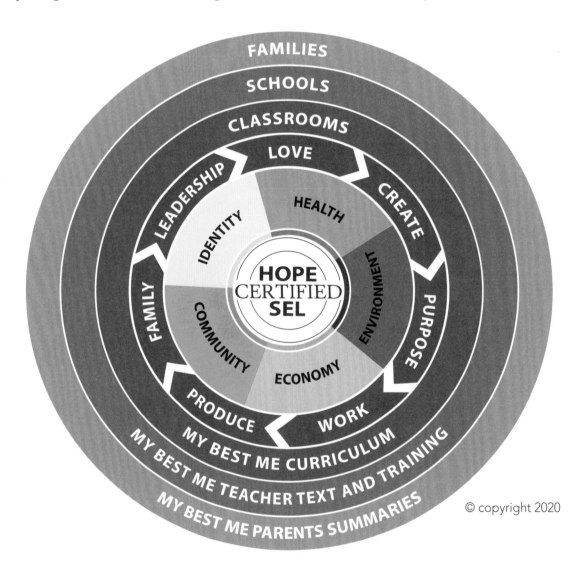

© copyright 2020

teamwork • willpower • leadership • goal setting • growth mindset • problem solving
time management • reasoning skills • organizing skills • strategic thinking • conflict resolution
willingness to learn • creative thinking • stress management • finance management
communication skills • emotional intelligence • nonverbal communication

Competencies

In the text, you will find five units that form the building blocks of a society, which will be used to train students. They will facilitate the use of this book.

IDENTITY
Discover who I am

My role
My personality
My character

HEALTH
Discover how to maintain order

Physical
Mental
Emotional

COMMUNITY
Discover how to interact with others

Family
People like me
People different from me
Strangers

ENVIRONMENT
Discover why and how to
manage nature

Natural resources
Plant life
Animal life

ECONOMICS
Discover the difference between
wealth, value, and true success

Needs versus wants
Financial balance
Resource management

Understanding The Icons

 READ

A story, a poem, a saying or a script that adds to the subject

 APPLY

To bring into action, put to use, and demonstrate understanding

 UNDERSTAND

To gain knowledge, insight, and understanding through information

 GIFT

A contribution, present or surprise to share with others

 OBSERVE

To look, see, find, watch, and discover more

 ACTIVITY

A task that involves direct experience and action

 CREATE

To paint, color or make in a personal way

 COMMENT

Discuss, consider, or examine certain subjects

 GAME

Engage in en experiment and discovery together

 REFLECT

Think, ponder, meditate or wonder about important issues

 WRITE

To write, mark, or sketch personal ideas or discoveries

 MUSIC

To learn, write, sing or listen to a song; enjoy a harmony of sounds

 CONCLUSION

A closing on the lesson subject with a final thought

 VIDEO

Watch a clip or film section and analyze the information

Contents

Identity

Health

Community

Environment

Economy

NOTES

IDENTITY

Discover who you are, what personality you were born with, how to become the best person you can be, and key roles in your life.

Having a clear sense of who you are as a person helps you become strong and confident.

It allows you to be a person who is not easily swayed by the circumstances or pressures of life.

It allows you to use your very own leadership qualities to make a difference on the world with who you are.

Why My Best Me?

Goal To discover the power of HOPE and why I need it

Pathways

Comment

What is one force you will need in life to be successful?

Why do you think this force is so important?

Write

When your desire for something is strong, the hope inside you will find a way to realize that desire. Want + Way + Will = Wellbeing.

Look at page 3 and fill in the words that are used for

Want: ___ ___ ___ ___

Way: ___ ___ ___ ___ ___ ___ ___ ___

Will: ___ ___ ___ ___ ___ ___ ___ ___ ___

Wellbeing: ___ ___ ___ ___

impossible
unable
unsolved
undoable

Understand

Hope is a very important power within you, because it helps you believe in a better tomorrow, no matter what. It also helps you speak about a better tomorrow, plan for a better tomorrow and then, take actions toward that better tomorrow.

Activity - Let's Rock the World

Select a rock; one that you found or a rock your teacher offers you. Decorate your rock into a beautiful reminder of inspiration for when times are hard and difficult. Your rock will be part of

the classroom "rock garden" with the purpose of encouraging you and your classmates to believe that anything is possible.

Apply

These lessons talk about very personal things or what we would call private information, like dreams, beliefs, fears, pains, struggles, and much more. It is important that each student avoids talking about what other classmates share. Your teacher will ask everyone in your class to sign a <u>Confidentiality</u> Agreement. That means that everyone promises to actively participate in class, be kind, thoughtful, trustworthy and wise. You are encouraged to sign this Confidentiality Agreement as a pledge to your peers and teacher that you are will always help build hope.

Video: 4yu.info/?i=93011

Watch this video to understand how small things can have a king-size impact. It will give you hope as you discover how important you are and how the world is waiting for your ideas.

4yu.info/?i=93011

Reflect

Here are some very important pieces to the HOPE puzzle:

1. You need to feel loved and valued. Who really loves you?
2. You need to know who you are. What makes you so special?
3. You need to know why you are alive. What can you give to help someone else?
4. You need to feel you belong somewhere. Where do you fit in?
5. You need to know you can become anything you want. What is something you dream of being or doing?

Willpower

Hope is my anchor. It helps me set goals, find pathways, grow my willpower and succeed.

The Bond of Family

Goal

Pathways

To understand the value of a family

Observe

Write

What do these two animal families have in <u>common</u>?

_____

What is the purpose of a family?

_____

What would happen if families didn't exist?

_____

Comment

There are many different types of families.

Describe how families are different.

Tell a partner about your family.

Understand

Many creatures on Earth form families because they perform important functions that allow them to exist. For humans, the family is the center of our society and a very important building block for strong communities. A family should supply love and care, protection, support, direction, examples, kind words and much more. Each member has a <u>role</u> inside the family. For example, parents give <u>instructions</u>, brothers and sisters share and assist each other, and older family members may share family history and wisdom. One thing is for sure; all family members learn from one another because of the <u>bond</u> between them.

Create - Present your family

Draw, color, cut and paste photos, or use other creative ways to show your family.

In groups of three, <u>compare</u> your families. Write down what you noticed on a sheet of paper. Share your answers with the class.

Reflect

What makes my family special?
How will my family change as I grow up?
What type of family would I like to have in the future?

I value my family. They are part of who I am.

Together Is Better!

Goal To learn the value and satisfaction of working with others

Pathways

Game - Let's race!

This game is best done outside or in a hallway. Instructions for a three-legged race:

- Choose a partner.
- Stand with your partner on one side.
- Use a <u>bandanna</u> to tie your right foot to your partner's left foot.
- When your teacher says go, run across the room with your partner.
- Have fun!

Comment

Would you have gone faster by yourself? Why?

What did you need to adjust to be able to run together with your partner? How?

Was it hard to do this activity? Why?

Understand

Let's imagine how life would be if everyone had the same interests and abilities with the same strengths and weaknesses. That would make life pretty boring and it would be impossible to help each other! The best way to work together is to <u>consider</u> others' strengths and <u>skills,</u> and agree on how to work together as a team. Working as a group is a give-and-take process that takes understanding, time and patience. When we participate in a team activity, we notice that each person has their own way of doing things. Sometimes we need to work through our differences in order to <u>succeed</u>.

4yu.info/?i=93021

Video:

How did the
<u>meerkats</u> work together to
get the fruit back? Could they have
done it on their own? What happens
when one meerkat tries to do it
alone? 4yu.info/?i=93021

 Activity

- Form groups of four and <u>distribute</u> these
  tasks: 1. Drawer 2. Colorer 3. Gluer 4. Time
  manager
- You will have 20 minutes to complete this
  project.
- On a large piece of construction paper, draw
  a tree and four pieces of fruit.
- Color the tree.
- Glue dry or fresh leaves to the branches.
- Make four pieces of fruit.
- Each person in the group will write their task
  or responsibility on a piece of fruit.

Reflect

Was the group activity difficult? Why?

What part of the project did I like the most? Why?

What are my abilities and skills? Was I able to use these skills during the project?

Did I help others with their job or could I have helped in other ways? How?

Willpower

When I work with others, we add all of our unique strengths
together, giving us all success and <u>satisfaction</u>.

4 Words Heal or Hurt

Goal To learn to think before I speak and choose my words with great care

Pathways

Observe

Look at the two different situations:

1. Steven takes his time to answer the questions on his test.
2. Steven takes little or no time to answer his sister.

Comment

Is there a difference in Steven's <u>behavior</u>?

Why does Steven take time to think before he answers the test questions?

Why does Steven answer his sister so quickly?

Understand

Steven thought carefully how to answer the questions on his test because he wanted a good grade. He did not take much time to think about how to answer his sister and how his answer would <u>affect</u> her.

The way we respond and the words we use affect others much more than we can see on the outside. When we speak in a <u>harsh</u> way and use mean words, we harm others and our relationship with them. If we think before we speak, use <u>encouraging</u> words

that heal and build others up, and communicate kindly,
we help others experience peace and joy in their life as well
as in our life. These types of actions usually cause friendly responses.

Video: 4yu.info/?i=93031

Why do children make fun of other children?
What do you feel when others make fun of you?
Why do you think it hurt Bird when Bernice
posted the mean picture of her?
What should Bird do so Bernice stops saying
mean things about her?

4yu.info/?i=93031

Write

What is a friendly way to respond to the following situations?

- A classmate: "I will not let you use my pencils!"
  Me: "_____"

- My mom: "Go clean up your room!"
  Me: "_____"

- A friend: "We will play what I want!"
  Me: "_____"

- A teacher: "Your notebook is a mess!"
  Me: "_____"

Reflect

What happens when you respond to others in a friendly way?
Do you think before you answer your parents? Your friends?
Is there a difference in how you respond to your friends and parents? Why?
Are you friendly to the strangers that help you (bus driver, cashier, server)?

Willpower

I choose <u>courteous</u> and friendly words when I speak to others.

Goal To find joy in being who I am at this time in my life

Pathways

Observe

Here is the <u>life cycle</u> of a frog.

Read the names of each <u>stage</u> out loud.

Egg

Tadpole

Adult frog

Young frog or froglet

Tadpole with legs

Comment

What do you notice about the frog's life cycle?

What <u>characteristics</u> do you notice in each stage?

Which stage do you find the most interesting? Why?

Can the frog skip a stage to grow faster? Why or why not?

Understand

Like the frog, all creatures have a life cycle and go through different growing stages. Human beings also go through different <u>phases</u> as they <u>mature</u>: <u>infancy</u>, childhood, <u>adolescence</u>, adulthood, and old age. Each stage follows another and is unique, due to changes in each new stage. Though men and women change in different ways, they all go through the same life stages. It doesn't matter what stage of life we are in, the important thing is to enjoy it!

Observe

Look at the image and describe the different characteristics you believe go with each life phase.

Infancy   Childhood   Adolescence   Adulthood   Old Age

Game

Can you guess which stage of life I represent? Without telling your classmates which one, act out a stage of the human life cycle. Your classmates will guess which stage you are acting out.

Video: 4yu.info/?i=93051

Watch this video and see how valuable life is no matter which stage you are in. We are who we are because of others who took the time to love us and care for us.

4yu.info/?i=93051

Reflect

What differences are there between a child, an adult, and an elderly person?
Does an individual behave the same way in each different stage of life?
In which stage of life are you? How are you feeling about this stage of your life?
What things can you do as a child that you cannot do when you are an adult?

Willpower

I **value** all stages of life and **purposefully** enjoy them all.

6 I Know When to Say "NO"

Goal To learn that saying "no" can be the right way to take care of myself

Pathways

Read "Nela and the Cake"

One day, Nela's aunt baked a cake for her. It looked delicious. Nela sat down and enjoyed a giant piece of cake that her aunt had cut for her. When she finished, her aunt said, "Here, have another piece." Nela was already full, but she did not want to say "no" to her aunt, so she took the cake and began to eat it. After eating half of her second piece of cake, Nela felt like she could not eat anymore. Her aunt said, "Don't waste the delicious cake that I made for you. Why don't you finish that piece?" So Nela finished the piece of cake. After finishing the cake, Nela felt very sick. She ate too much cake! Now she was too full and had a stomach ache.

Comment

What happened to Nela?
Why was her stomach hurting?
Could Nela have avoided feeling sick? How?

Understand

Often we accept invitations to participate in things that could be harmful to us. That is what happened to Nela. Clear limits or boundaries help us to respect and care for ourselves.

There are moments when we have an <u>internal</u> voice or a "<u>hunch</u>" that tells us to not do or accept something someone offers us. It is important to pay <u>attention</u> to that inner voice. When we want to set <u>limits</u>, it should be enough to say, "No, thank you." However, if our answer is not accepted by the other person, then we can, in a <u>polite</u> way, walk away from the situation.

Observe

Reflect

What would I do in a <u>similar</u> situation?

What emotion do I sense when I know I should say "no" but I do not do so?

Do I know my limits? An example of a limit in my life is...

_____

Am I brave enough to firmly say "no" and stick with it, especially in difficult situations where I feel <u>pressure</u>? Please explain.

What do I do if I <u>lack</u> the <u>courage</u> to say "no"?

Willpower

I care for myself by knowing when and how to say "no" in a <u>confident</u> and kind manner.

Upward Every Day

Goal

To <u>recognize</u> that I can learn from others

Pathways

 Comment

What does the word "<u>humble</u>" mean?

 Create

Use modeling clay to create a tree in 10 minutes.

 Comment

Were you able to finish creating the tree during the time allowed?
How did your tree turn out? Was it easy to <u>mold</u> the clay? Why?
What would you have experienced if you had <u>carved</u> it out of wood?
What would you have experienced if you had sculpted a tree out of a rock?

 Understand

During our life, we are formed and shaped by the people and situations around us. However, that process of formation can be easily done like the molding of a lump of clay, or difficult like the carving of a piece of wood, or the sculpting of a stone. Just like the tree, we are either molded, carved or <u>sculpted</u> by the people around us who play a part in our growth. Our <u>attitude</u> decides how we are going to be developed and taught by others. The key is to have a humble and <u>modest</u> attitude (not negative or bossy), yet strong enough to stand up for our values and <u>morals</u>. A humble and

modest person is someone who is:

1. Aware that he/she needs help and can ask for it boldly
2. Focused on other people
3. Helpful, kind and responsible in all he/she does
4. Led by morals and values
5. Thankful and grateful even in difficult situations
6. Open to receiving instructions and corrections
7. Ready to admit his/her mistakes and is willing to ask forgiveness.

Think about a humble and modest person you know. Are there other ways to describe them? What are they?

_____   _____   _____   _____

 Observe

Look at the first image. How would you react? Circle one of the last two images.

 **Reflect**

Describe the image you circled.

Why did you pick that image?

What is the best way to respond to the instructions of your teachers, parents or caregivers?

Why is it healthier for you to be flexible and open to new ideas?

 **Willpower**

I am <u>flexible</u> and listen to what others say, so I can learn from them.

NOTES

Health

Discover how to grow and thrive physically, mentally, emotionally, and socially by keeping order and balance in your life.

Consistently maintain your health to increase your energy level, protect you against disease, and improve your overall appearance and mental outlook.

Your health is an important building block to you reaching your goals and living a life of satisfaction, overflowing with happiness and strong self-worth.

My Health Begins with Me

8

Goal To understand that my choices greatly <u>influence</u> my overall health and <u>well-being</u>

Pathways

Game

- Choose a piece of paper from a bag.
- Look at your piece of paper: if it has the name of a bug, call it out.
- The person who is "the bug" will try to "sting" the others by tagging them.
- If the "bug" classmate touches other classmates, they will act as if they are stung and sit down. They are "out."
- When all players have been "<u>stung,</u>" the game is over and a new round can start, using a different "bug."

Comment

What did you do when the "bug" person was near?

In life, what measures do you take to avoid being "stung" by sickness or disease?

Who's decisions have the greatest <u>affect</u> on your health? Please explain.

Understand

In the game, if a player ran away, he or she did not get stung. To get stung by a bug would mean you lost and would be out of the game. This is what happens in life: when we are "stung" with sickness it keeps us from being involved in all of the activities that we enjoy and cuts us off from other people.

The decisions we make each day play a role in whether
or not we have a cheerful or gloomy attitude. For example,
we choose what, when, and how much to eat. We choose when and
how we rest, who to hang out with, what we believe, and what we do in our free
time. If the decisions we make are <u>damaging,</u> we will experience the <u>consequences</u>.
However, if we take responsibility for our decisions and want to care for our health, we
will make positive choices, seeing positive results as we grow.

Create a <u>Menu</u>

Let's focus on our food decisions. Few things affect us faster
than the foods we decide to eat. Use a food pyramid (link:
flives.us/?i=93081) and with a partner ...

- Think about your favorite meal and create a menu describing
the food in that meal.
- After you have created your menu, share it with a partner.
- When talking with your partner, share the reasons for your
choices. Use the questions below to guide your <u>conversation</u>.

Reflect

Did you and your partner create complete, <u>balanced</u>, and satisfying meal?
Is the meal healthy? Please explain.
What would be an unhealthy meal? Give at least one example.
What would happen if you ate an unhealthy dinner every night?
How do you feel when you eat a healthy meal?
How do you feel when you eat an unhealthy meal?
What are some of the long-term effects of eating poorly?
What other constructive aspects are related to food?

Willpower

**I am responsible for my health and will <u>improve</u>
my meal choices.**

The Kaleidoscope of Health

Goal To learn that my health is related to many different areas of my life

Pathways

 Understand

When we are healthy, we can live our lives with energy and <u>enthusiasm</u>. Though this sounds easy, the truth is that health is a <u>complex</u> issue that has to do with many areas of life including our bodies, our minds, our <u>emotions</u>, our schools and our <u>environment</u>. All these areas are <u>knit</u> together with the daily choices we make, and they all play a role in how we feel and how we experience life.

 Draw - On the following lists, circle the healthy things you do each day.

With my body: Keep myself clean, drink at least 8 glasses of water, eat a balanced diet, sleep at least 8 hours, play outside, exercise.

With my mind: Do my school work, read books, play games, do puzzles, draw, learn to play an instrument, sing, create an <u>invention</u>, cook, build, <u>design</u>.

With my <u>relationships</u> with others: Obey my parents and teachers, spend time with my friends, visit family, <u>volunteer</u> in my community, share my things, help others, give <u>compliments</u>, <u>encourage</u> others, show my <u>affection</u>, give gifts, greet those around me, say "please" and "thank you."

With my inner self: Be thankful, be <u>forgiving</u>, listen to good music, sit alone and think, be caring, make wise decisions, help others, be honest, be nice to someone who is not friendly, journal, take a stand for what I believe in.

 Comment

<u>Review</u> the activities you did not mark.

28

Do you think these activities are healthy? Why or why not?

Which activities do you plan to add to your daily life? Why?

What other healthy things do you do that are not on the list?

Game

- Form a circle with your classmates. The teacher will tell you where to go.
- Your teacher will start the game and will name something healthy.
- The next student in line will use the last letter of that word and mention another healthy thing until the last student shares. For example: If the teacher says "vegetables" the next student will use the letter S and may say "sleep," and then the next one uses the P for "play," etc.

Create

Make a poster about you! Gather different colored square pieces of paper. On each piece of paper write a word that has to do with healthy activities that you do. Write down one <u>detailed</u> action with each word. For example Water: 8 glasses/day. In the middle of a large piece of poster paper, 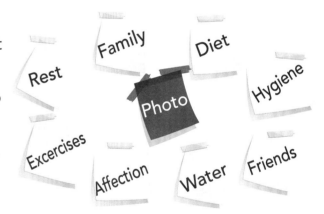 glue a picture of yourself. Around your picture, glue the written words. See the example. <u>Decorate</u> your poster to emphasize how healthy you are.

Reflect

The poster project will remind you that you are responsible for your health. Hang this on the wall of your bedroom, the refrigerator, or in the classroom to help you reflect on your daily decisions and habits.

Willpower

I live with purpose! I develop healthy habits for my life!

Clean Mind, Content Life

Goal To learn that taking care of how I feel on the inside is as important as taking care of the outside

Pathways

 Comment

What makes you happy? Write down five things that make you happy. (It could be a favorite place, an activity, a person, etc.)

1. _____
2. _____
3. _____
4. _____
5. _____

Compare your list with your classmates. Did any of you have the same ideas?

 Understand

We clean our bodies regularly in order to stay healthy. Did you know that it is just as important to keep our thoughts and feelings "clean?" We will thrive in every area of our lives when we keep our minds at peace, our hearts <u>content</u>, we are <u>generous</u> and <u>pleasant</u> with friends, and always have something positive to say to others.

Sometimes, things happen that make us feel sad or angry, or we can say words or do things that hurt someone's feelings, maybe without realizing it. These situations can turn into more serious problems if they are not quickly handled. Talking about the way you feel and why you feel that way can help keep your mind and heart "clean." Telling someone that you are <u>sorry</u> for hurting them and asking for forgiveness are two ways to care for yourself. How do you feel when you say sorry? How do you feel when someone says sorry to you?

Video: 4yu.info/?i=93091
Watch, "Have You Filled A Bucket Today?"

Apply
Create a small bucket out of a sheet of paper. Write a positive note to a classmate and place it in their bucket. Read some of the notes as a class, or post them on the bulletin board.

4yu.info/?i=93091

Create
Make a series of index cards titled "I Feel Healthy on the Inside." On each card, draw a picture, write some words, paste photos, and/or pictures that describe what makes your mind and heart feel healthy. You may list actions, such as saying "sorry" if you hurt someone, reading books, listening to music, thinking of a person who has had a positive <u>impact</u> on your life, writing out your thoughts and dreams, etc.

After sharing your cards with some classmates, take them home and place them somewhere as a daily reminder of the choices you can make to guard your mind and heart from negative influences. It will help you remember that staying healthy involves more than just brushing your teeth and washing your hands.

Reflect
What can I do today to feel healthy on the inside?

_____

_____

Willpower

I choose to be grateful and keep my mind and heart clean, so I can be healthy on the inside as well as on the outside.

11

This Will Grow Your Mind

Goal To learn that I have the power to make myself smarter

Pathways

Understand

Did you know that you can make yourself smarter? Our brains act like muscles; they get stronger with more use. Challenging our brain to do something, makes it sharp. Dr. Carol Dweck discovered that the only thing that limits our brain is when we say, "I can't." We should always choose to use the words, "I can do this." If we study, practice and stretch our brains, we will become smarter. We should decide to never give up on anything we want to do or learn.

A Growth Mindset is when we believe that our brain is able to learn and do anything we tell it to do. A <u>Fixed Mindset</u> is when a person believes that they are limited in how smart they can be.

A person with a Fixed Mindset believes that if they fail in a certain task, they will always fail in that task. A person with a <u>Growth Mindset</u> believes that with a lot of practice and an <u>optimistic</u> attitude, they can improve and get better at any task. They "believe in the power of yet." Let's listen to the book below to learn about "the power of yet" as Julia Cook explains what Dr. Dweck is talking about.

Video: 4yu.info/?i=93101
Take a moment to look at this clip

Comment

What were some <u>challenges</u> Brick Brain faced?

4yu.info/?i=93101

32

Did Bubble Gum Brain treat challenges differently?

Have you ever behaved like Brick Brain? Please explain.

Have you behaved like Bubble Gum Brain? Please explain.

What was the most important thing Brick Brain learned at the end of the story?

Activity

What is your <u>talent</u>? Singing? Basketball? Drawing? Or are you well informed about a certain subject that interests you? Share that talent and/or information with your classmates by holding a "<u>mini</u> <u>workshop</u>" in class, teaching others your skill, talent or knowledge. The class will form groups small enough so every <u>participant</u> can learn and practice something new. Be sure to join a group that is teaching something you do not know, not know how to do or cannot do well... yet! Take time each week to attend your mini workshop.

Write

Create a "not yet, but I will" <u>statement</u> (e.g., "I don't know how to .... yet, but I will practice .... daily to learn this new skill).

_____

_____

Reflect

Was it difficult to develop a "not yet" statement? Practice this "not yet" statement for 63 days and then come back to the classroom and tell everyone about your experience of using your Growth Mindset.

Repeat after me: "I Can do This"

Willpower

If I believe I can, I will. I believe I can always learn something new, so I will become smarter.

12 Outside Fun

Goal

To understand the health benefit of being active outdoors.

Pathways

Activity

Select a partner and complete the following steps:

Step 1

- Inflate a balloon and deflate it.
- Repeat this same action five times.
- Observe the characteristics of this balloon and write down your findings.

Step 2

- Inflate another balloon and tie off the end.
- Observe its characteristics and write down your observations.
- Play with the balloon for 5 minutes with your partner.

Comment

How did the balloon that was inflated and deflated 5 times look and feel?

How did the balloon that was inflated just once look and feel?

What balloon appears to be in better condition at the end of the activity? Why?

What is the purpose of balloons?

Understand

Balloons are made for having fun and decorating our surroundings. When we inflate and deflate a balloon time after time, we are not using it in the way it was meant to be used. We wear out the balloon by inflating and deflating it.

How do you feel when you do the same activity over and over again? For example, do you like watching the same TV show for many hours, or sitting in the same spot for a long time? Could we feel stretched and <u>strained</u> doing the same thing many times over? Just like the balloon needs to be used properly, our bodies need proper exercise and outdoor time.

We can change our <u>routine</u> by the simple decision to go outside daily; to play in the fresh air, planning new and <u>imaginative</u> adventures and trips. These actions will give us fresh energy and help us feel strong and healthy. There is a new world to <u>explore</u> every day! We will benefit more from life when we whole-heartedly decide to enjoy each moment, each corner of our planet and every beautiful creature in nature. This will help us take care of our bodies, both inside and out.

Draw

Create a picture of your favorite outdoor place.

Reflect

How many times a week do you go outside to enjoy outdoor life?

How many hours do you spend sitting inside on a couch, bed, or chair?

How many of those hours inside are you in front of a screen?

What are your favorite outdoor activities?

Is there a new place you'd like to explore that is outside?

Willpower

I spend time outside to refresh myself and keep myself healthy.

13 Swimming Upstream

Goal — To learn to act with courage, even when everything seems to be going against me

Pathways

Read - The Courageous Salmon

Have you ever seen video clips of salmon leaping upstream? They make an <u>incredible</u> trip against the <u>current</u> and some <u>survive</u> against all <u>odds</u>. Scientists are still <u>amazed</u> by their <u>unique</u> abilities.

Salmon are born in the fresh cold waters of fast-flowing rivers. Once they are a little older, they head out to sea and live there until they become adults. When the time comes to have babies, they return to the river where they were born. The trip back is very hard and full of many difficulties. The salmon must swim through <u>raging</u> <u>rapids</u> and waterfalls. They have to survive hitting the rocks in the rapids time and time again, free themselves from plants when they get stuck, and escape from countless <u>predators</u> who want to eat them, including grizzly bears! The salmon are willing to risk everything to realize their designed purpose. They must overcome many obstacles to reach their <u>destiny</u> and experience something <u>magnificent</u>. They refuse to give up!

It is important for each of us to "swim against the current" as well, especially when it is difficult. It requires strength, energy, <u>persistence</u> and <u>determination</u> (or <u>grit</u>) to do the right thing, even when other people and <u>circumstances</u> may be against us. We must act with courage to make difficult decisions and follow through with our plan.

4yu.info/?i=93121

36

Video: "Grizzly Bears Catching Salmon."

4yu.info/?i=93121 Watch the video,

Did you find yourself <u>rooting</u> for the bears or the salmon?

How is your life, like that of the salmon? Please explain.

 Comment

Mark the statements that you can <u>relate</u> to with an (X), and answer the questions.

____ My friends plan to do something that I know is wrong.

____ My mom asks me to be obedient, even when the rest of my friends are not.

____ A classmate teases me, and does not believe I can do a good job.

____ I help someone, even when it is not the easiest thing to do.

____ When I am not good at something, I give up.

____ My homework is too difficult, so I don't finish.

Give an example of when you "swam against the current?"

_____

Have you followed the current (gone with the flow)? How did you feel afterward?

_____

 Activity

Make a fish with colored paper, using the origami technique. Put the fish where you can see it every day. Let it remind you to be persistent and follow your dreams. Help each other fold the fish.

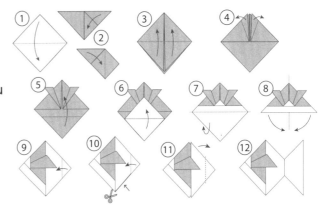

 **Reflect**

Why is it important to courageously decide to do the things that go against what everyone else is doing?

 **Willpower**

I am brave as I make right decisions, even if I am the only one. I have grit!

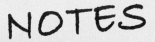

NOTES

COMMUNITY

Discover how to get along with others, those who are like you or different from you, and how to do your part in society in a healthy and positive way.

The people around you improve your life and give you a sense of belonging. Together with others you can do greater things, have more fun and become better at what you do. Serving others by sharing yourself through your skills, talents and personality will make your life better and give you great satisfaction. Being a part of community also gives you a "team beside you" that will root you on and help you be the best person you can be.

14 Faithful Friend

Goal

To learn that a friend is <u>faithful</u>

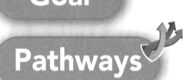
Pathways

Read

After you read the story, put each part in the correct order from 1 to 3

_____ The teacher never appeared, but Hachiko waited 10 years for him until he was no longer able to travel to the station. Today, there is a statue of Hachiko at the train station as an example of faithfulness.

_____ There once was a teacher in Japan who <u>adopted</u> a puppy and called him Hachiko. Every day, the dog would accompany the teacher to the train station and wait there for his return. After a year, the affection between the teacher and Hachiko had grown very strong. They were the best of friends.

_____ One afternoon, the teacher did not get off the train. He had passed away. However, day after day, not minding the weather, Hachiko appeared at the station waiting for the teacher.

Now read the story from the beginning to the end.

Comment

Why is it said that a dog is man's best friend?
What problems did Hachiko have to face?
How did he show he was a faithful friend?
What do you think of when you hear the word faithful?

Understand

Hachiko was a faithful dog because he was <u>devoted</u> and true to his friend. He loved his owner and he did not let circumstances of the weather or time influence his actions. Someone who is faithful is <u>sincere</u> and <u>reliable</u>, <u>loyal</u> and <u>trustworthy</u>. Faithfulness <u>implies</u> <u>dedication</u> and devotion. It means standing up for another person, a cause, an idea or a belief, even when it is difficult to do so.

Create

You will draw the name of one classmate out of a hat. Shhhhh!!!! Don't say the name out loud! Write letters in all capitals and then cut and paste them on a self-made card or piece of paper in order to create a secret, positive message for that student. Even if this person is not a close friend, encourage each other and stand by one another as classmates. Find <u>affirmative</u> things to say about your classmate and let them know through this secret message! Give the message to your teacher and he or she will pass it out to the correct person.

Reflect

Was it hard for you to create this message? Why or why not?

How did you feel when you read the message written to you?

Please give an example of you being faithful to a friend or family member.

How can you commit to being more faithful? Write down three ideas.

1. _____

2. _____

3. _____

Video: 4yu.info/?i=93131

Here is another story about a faithful dog. Watch this clip and be inspired to be a faithful friend.

4yu.info/?i=93131

I am always faithful to my friends and family.

Respect in the Classroom

Goal To learn to respect the learning environment in my classroom

 Comment

Read the words in the table below and circle the words that describe you. Explain why.

nice	respectful	<u>gentle</u>
helpful	considerate	polite
kind	warm and friendly	thoughtful
open	interested in others' ideas	accepting of others

 Read - My Classmates

My classmates are cool, there is no one I want to <u>insult</u>,
    I prefer to treat them **nicely**, <u>**attentively**</u>, and **politely**.
I like my classmates, I don't want to bother them,
    I prefer to be **helpful**, <u>**considerate**</u> and <u>**gentle**</u>.
My classmates are cool, there is no one I want to anger or hurt,
    I prefer to be **kind**, **friendly**, and **thoughtful**.
I like my classmates, I don't want to <u>judge</u> and <u>criticize</u>,
    I want to be **open**, **interested**, and **accepting**.

 Write

Create your own sentences with at least six of the highlighted words and share them with the class. If you don't know the meaning, look it up.

_____

_____

_____

_____

_____

_____

Understand

How we behave during class has a direct effect on others around us. It is easy to get distracted, and if we are not respectful, we disrupt other's effort to learn. If we are mindful, kind, quiet, talk in turn, and listen to others, we can learn from one another.

Activity - The traffic light of respect

- Three colored poster boards will be placed on the wall:

    Red: Behavior that shows no respect

    Yellow: Behavior that shows little respect

    Green: Behavior that shows respect

- In your group (3-5), brainstorm a list of classroom behaviors. Write the behaviors on the colored slips of paper you received that corresponds to the colored poster board.

- Post your slips of paper on the wall under the correct color.

Draw

Write your promised behavior on a piece of paper. In the classroom I promise to:

_____

Name: _____ Signature: _____

Reflect

Have I had moments in which I lacked respect for my teacher and classmates? How can I be more helpful and useful in my learning environment?

Willpower

I want everyone in my class to be able to learn. I will respect my classroom learning environment.

In Your Shoes

Goal 🏆 To learn to put myself in someone else's shoes

Pathways

Game

What am I?

- Choose a piece of paper out of the hat and silently read the name of the animal written on the paper.
- Without sound, act out the animal you picked in front of the class.
- The class will guess which animal you are acting out.

Who am I?

- Choose a piece of paper out of the hat and silently read the student's name written on the paper.
- Write down three positive <u>descriptions</u> about your classmate and two things your classmate likes and give to the teacher.
- The teacher will read your description to the class, (keeping their name secret).

  "I am _____, _____, and _____."

  "I like _____ and _____."
- The class will guess who you described.

💬 Comment

While acting, did you feel like the animal? Did you <u>represent</u> your classmate well?

Did your classmates guess which animal you were?

Did your classmates guess which student you described?

Which of the two presentations was easier for you to do?

Understand

Life is fun and interesting because we are all different. We have different interests, a variety of <u>styles</u>, <u>distinct</u> <u>cultures</u> and beliefs, and unique <u>personalities</u>. <u>Empathy</u> and <u>compassion</u> are skills that we need when we relate to others. Empathy is when we understand the difficulties others face every day, what they like or what bothers them, and why they act and react the way they do in each situation. Compassion is when we show them sincere love and are gentle in how we react.

4yu.info/?i=93151

Video: 4yu.info/?i=93151

What can empathy bring to you?

Why did the young man help those people?

What did he get out of it? What did they receive?

Activity - Buddy Challenge

1. Mark from the list the three things that bother you the most:

- [ ] Someone takes my supplies out without my permission.
- [ ] Someone breaks my supplies.
- [ ] Someone calls me nicknames.
- [ ] Being pushed in line.
- [ ] Being blamed for something I didn't do.
- [ ] Someone doesn't do what I ask.
- [ ] Being hit.
- [ ] Being screamed at.
- [ ] Being lied to.
- [ ] Not being answered.
- [ ] Not being listened to.
- [ ] Other: _____

2. Read your dislikes to a classmate.

3. Lookup the words "empathy" and "compassion" in the dictionary.

4. For the rest of the day, watch out for your buddy. Show empathy and compassion when things they don't like happen to them. Make sure you help your buddy.

Reflect

Does everyone like and dislike the same things?

Were you able to help your partner today? How?

Can you understand your classmate better after recognizing his or her dislikes?

Willpower

My empathy for my classmates deepens and develops as I better understand them.

I Can Help!

Goal To learn that I am <u>capable</u> of helping others

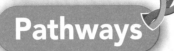

Observe

What is happening in the <u>maze</u>?

Draw yourself in the empty box.

With your pencil, trace each road and find out

who is closest to help the girl on crutches.

Comment

Who was closest to helping the girl?

Can you help someone you don't know? How?

How do you feel after you help someone?

Have you received help from someone you never expected or knew?

Understand

We all have the ability to help others and should be willing to do so. There are many ways to help others; we only need to use our creativity, consideration, and courage to do so. We can <u>lend</u> a helping hand, <u>donate</u> money, offer our time, our skills, our strength,

give a word of encouragement, <u>accompany</u> others
in difficult moments, or visit the sick. Sometimes the person
who needs and receives our help can feel <u>uncomfortable</u> or <u>ashamed</u>.
Have you ever felt too scared or ashamed to ask for help? It is important that when
we offer our help, we do it with <u>sensitivity</u> toward the other person's feelings.

Video - Watch: Color Your World With Kindness
How did the characters help each other and
show kindness?
What is one small act of kindness you can do today?
4yu.info/?i=93161

4yu.info/?i=93161

Observe

Underneath each image, and in one word, write a creative idea of how to help

_____ _____ _____ _____

Reflect

Have you ever needed someone's help? Did you ask for help or was it given to you without
asking? How did it feel to receive help? Is it hard to help others? Why? How can you
practice helping others? Write three ways you will help a friend or family member this week.

1. _____
2. _____
3. _____

I am considerate, courageous, and creative in helping
others.

Let's Talk About It

Goal

To learn to solve conflicts calmly

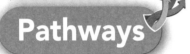
Pathways

Activity

In small groups, untangle the rope you were given.

Comment

Who was able to untangle it first?

Did you use a <u>strategy</u> to <u>untangle</u> the rope? Please explain.

Did you like untangling the rope?

Did your classmates in your group like untangling the rope?

Who was the best at untangling the rope in your group? Why?

Was it better to untangle it calmly or to try to hurry and finish first?

Read

Julio has several pencils in his desk. Emily doesn't have a pencil to do her homework, so she goes over to Julio's desk and takes one without asking. She returns to her desk while Julio runs over to her desk and <u>yanks</u> it out of her hands.

Comment

In this story, was there anyone at fault? Please explain.

How would you solve the problem(s) presented in this story?

How could the problem(s) presented have been avoided?

If you had this experience, what would you have done? Why?

Understand

If we were <u>anxious</u>, irritated or in a hurry when we untangled the rope, we probably tangled it more. If the girl in the drawing combs her hair quickly and impatiently, it will really hurt her and she will make little or no progress.

Conflicts with classmates and friends are like knots and tangles, and they should be approached and solved in the same way; little by little and with patience. It is a healthy habit to talk about our conflicts. When we take the time to solve a conflict, we should give each person involved the opportunity to share his/her thoughts. Then, we should recognize what the other person said, decide on the best solution, and apply it. At times, we may need a referee to help us come to an agreement.

Activity

- Form a group of five.
- Make 2 teams of 2 and the 5th person will be a moderator (referee).
- You will be given an example of a classroom conflict by your teacher.
- Practice discussing and resolving the conflict in a calm way.
- Present your experience to the class.

Reflect

Is it easier to resolve conflicts with a referee? Why?

Is it easier to be calm or show anger?

Am I able to solve problems when I am anxious?

How do I remain calm when I feel irritated? List three ways.

1. _____
2. _____
3. _____

Willpower

I will resolve conflicts by listening to others and using calm words.

19 I Do What I Say

Goal

To understand that others trust me when I do what I say I will do

Pathways

 Draw

Put the <u>phrase</u> in the correct order. Write the words in the <u>corresponding</u> boxes.

Do cannot keep that make promises not you

Do not make promises that you cannot keep

Define "<u>promise</u>" _____

Comment

What does the phrase on the train mean?
What is expected when you give your word? Why?
Have you ever made a promise and not kept it?
Has someone ever promised you something and
didn't follow through? How did you feel?

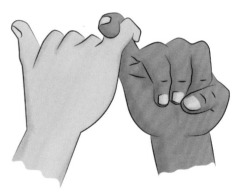

 Understand

What do you think of when you hear the word trust? To grow, mature, and have
an impact on others, we need people to trust us. Trust is something we <u>gain</u> over
time, when our words and actions match. Someone is <u>dependable</u> when they
do what they say. That is why we keep our promises no matter how unimportant
they may seem. This shows, in a powerful way, that we value ourselves and others
because we consider our words to be important.

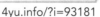

Video:

Watch the clip first and
then read the story.
4yu.info/?i=93181

Read

One day, a hungry lion caught a mouse to eat. The mouse begged: "Please, oh king of the animals, let me go! I am too small to still your hunger. If you let me go, one day I will be able to help you." The lion roared with laughter: "Help me, you weak, small creature? You <u>humored</u> me so I will not eat you." With that said, the lion let the mouse go. Time passed until one day the lion was caught in a thick net. He roared in anger but could not escape. The mouse heard his roar and knew the jungle king was in trouble. He ran as fast as he could to find the lion. Then with his teeth, the mouse started <u>gnawing</u> at the rope. He chewed, bit and <u>tugged</u> until it broke. At last, the lion was able to escape through the gap to freedom. That day, the mouse and the lion became good friends, with a trust that <u>endured</u> any <u>trial</u>.

Comment

Did the mouse keep his word?
How does this story help you understand the importance of trust?

Activity

Do you trust your classmates? How can you become more trustworthy? Meet in groups of 3-4 to talk about what trust means to you.

Reflect

Are you able to put your trust in your classmates? Why or why not?
How do I gain people's trust?

Willpower

I will be trustworthy, always keeping my word.

community

4yu.info/?i=93181

NOTES

ENVIRONMENT

Discover the value of managing and protecting your home, planet Earth, with all its resources.

Wisely protecting and managing Earth's resources is the key to making sure you have a beautiful, healthy and safe place to live, as well as for your children and all other living creatures.

Goal To learn that each creature plays an important role in the environment.

Draw

Complete these cycles by drawing what is missing in the <u>food</u> <u>chain</u>.

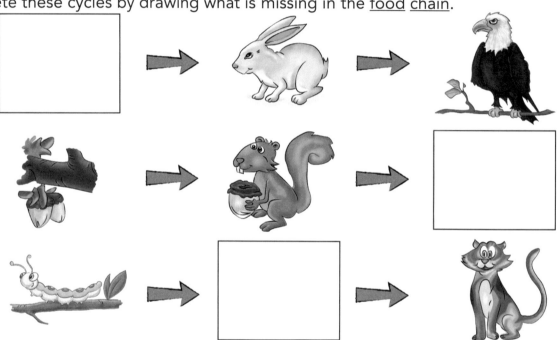

Comment

What would happen if there weren't any creatures that ate rabbits?

What would happen if <u>caterpillars</u> or acorns were not eaten by other creatures?

Where do you belong in the food chain?

Understand

Life is often presented as a circle because it seems to wrap around like a loop. When one creature dies it becomes a nutrition source for other living creatures, and therefore, produces life. In nature, each plant and every creature functions and has its place in the food and life cycles that exist. The grass has a life cycle of its own and, at the same time, is part of a greater cycle, in which it feeds the rabbits. The rabbits have their own cycle of <u>development</u>, yet they feed the eagle and, therefore, are part of a more <u>complex</u> life cycle. Each living creature is necessary and forms part of this beautiful world, which is sustained by these different life cycles.

We are also part of these life cycles, and because of our abilities, we use nature and its living creatures in far more <u>extensive</u> ways than just for food. We greatly profit from all the resources that are available in our environment to an <u>extent</u> that, if we are not careful, we can <u>endanger</u> those cycles. Therefore, people are the only creatures that have the full responsibility of caring for the natural environment in a wise and balanced way so that it will not be destroyed. We have the ability to carefully protect living creatures, their <u>habitats</u>, and their life cycles so that all of nature continues to operate and function. In this world where "the big eat the small," we, as the "biggest," should operate and manage these riches with great care.

Apply

Food Chains: Go on the Internet and do some research about food chains. With a partner, create a poster representing what you discovered. You may draw pictures, print them from the Internet, or cut them out of magazines.

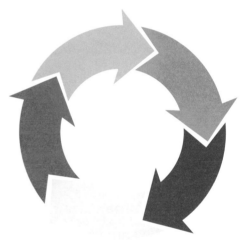

Reflect

What is my role inside the circles of life? Why am I valuable?
Have we done an <u>adequate</u> job of taking care of the natural environment? Why or why not?

Willpower

I take care of my natural environment to maintain the balance of all the life cycles around me.

Goal

To understand that when I am organized my productivity increases

Pathways

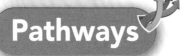

Read

The library is a very special place because it contains thousands of books. Daily, people visit the library to check out many different types of texts. With so many books, how do we find what we are looking for?

Create

Assign a category to each set of books and color the books with the appropriate color.

- Red: Science fiction
- Green: Fairy tales
- Yellow: Poetry
- Purple: History
- Blue: Dictionaries

Comment

Why are libraries so orderly and organized?

What would happen if the books were not shelved in an orderly fashion?

What other places are as orderly as the library?

Have you looked for something in your bedroom and weren't able to find it?

How much time did you lose trying to find it?

Understand

Look up the words "efficient" and "effective" in the dictionary. Certainly everything works in a more efficient and effective way when we follow a certain order and maintain a structure. An orderly and prepared place (space), a planned day (time), and a <u>consistent</u> <u>habit</u> (method) help us perform activities in an efficient way without experiencing the frustration of chaos. The way in which we maintain what surrounds us, how we organize our time and how we <u>accomplish</u> a task, <u>reflect</u> who we are. Our actions are the results of what we value. The <u>appearance</u> of our things is a <u>reflection</u> of our <u>organizational</u> skills. Keeping order shows that we care about ourselves and others.

Observe

Comment

Are there differences between these two classrooms?

Describe an orderly classroom compared to one that is disorderly and disorganized.

Which type of classroom do you <u>prefer</u>? Why?

Apply

In groups of 4, create a set of class rules that will help maintain an orderly classroom. Display rules that you will apply daily and follow in your classroom.

Reflect

How do I maintain my school supplies? My bedroom? My time? My classroom? In what ways can I improve my organizational skills?

Willpower

I organize my belongings, my time, and my method of working in order to live a more <u>productive</u> life.

22

Trash or Treasure?

Goal To learn to <u>re-purpose</u> objects and materials that I no longer need

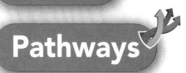

Pathways

Game

You have 3 minutes to write as many objects as you can think of that go in each trash bin. How many can you think of? Ready, set, go!!!

GLASS   PLASTIC   PAPER   METAL

_____ _____ _____ _____

_____ _____ _____ _____

_____ _____ _____ _____

_____ _____ _____ _____

_____ _____ _____ _____

Comment

Do you have any of these trash bins at your home? Which ones?

What is <u>recycling</u>? Look it up in the dictionary if you don't know.

Why would you recycle your trash?

Do you recycle at home? What gets recycled?

Name some <u>items</u> you no longer need that can be sold or reused.

Understand

There are many things we throw away because we do not like them any more, we no longer use them, or they are out of style. However, a great number of these items can be reused or <u>transformed</u> into other products that can be <u>profitable</u>, helpful, or fun to make. For example, glass bottles can be decorated and used as vases or piggy banks. Attractive jars and cardboard boxes can be creatively redesigned and used for storage. All this is possible when we are creative and motivated to start the process of reusing items that we would have otherwise thrown away. This subject also helps us think about creative solutions on how to deal with excessive amounts of trash in the environment.

Activity

What can you re-use?

Think outside the box!

Be an <u>inventor</u>! Make a treasure. Choose one trash item that you will turn into something new and try to use as many materials as possible that you would have otherwise defined as trash. Once you finish your new "invention," present it to the class.

Reflect

Do you think it is important to recycle? Why or why not?

Can you explain the title of the lesson, "Trash or Treasure"?

Did you enjoy re-purposing an item that would have otherwise been trash?

Were you able to make a treasure from trash?

Willpower

I realize that trash can be treasure because many items can be transformed and reused.

I Care for Animals

23

Goal To learn to be <u>mindful</u> of animals and take care of them wisely

Pathways

Draw - Helping a Pet

A pet is considered healthy and happy when its needs are met. Fill in the bubbles below with what you do or can do to keep a pet healthy.

Understand

Animals are living creatures that feel (body) and have emotions (senses). They can be wild (a wolf) or tame (a pet dog). To a certain extent, they depend on us to live, whether we care for them directly or indirectly. To care for animals is to make sure that they are treated kindly, looked after, and that others don't <u>mistreat</u> or abuse them. How we treat animals is often a reflection of how we treat people.

Comment

What do pets need that people need, too?

Do I need to have traits like gentleness, patience, friendliness, etc. with a pet? What other traits are important for <u>interacting</u> with a pet?

_____

Activity - Care Plan

Write a weekly plan for caring for a pet that you have (or want to have). Think about its baths, walks, food, games, rest, <u>vaccinations</u>, etc.

MONDAY	TUESDAY	WEDNESDAY	THURSDAY	FRIDAY	SATURDAY

 Reflect

Do I have time to care for a pet? What would happen to my pet if I forgot to care for it? What would I do with my pet if I went on a trip? Can I take full responsibility for caring for a pet? Why or why not? Will I always be kind and gentle with a pet or any other animal?

Video: 4yu.info/?i=93221
Watch a wonderful <u>inspirational</u> clip about a boy and his puppy.

4yu.info/?i=93221

I am mindful of my pets and other animals. I take responsibility for the care they need. It is enjoyable!

Amazing Energy

Goal To learn that there are various forms of energy in the world around me

Pathways

Read - What is Energy?

When we look around, we can see objects as well as creatures in motion. Have you ever wondered what allows them to move around? Movement is possible because of energy or <u>fuel</u>. We use energy for many things and in many different ways. Energy is <u>drawn</u> from the environment to benefit us in the things we do; for example, to <u>generate</u> electricity. Many things in our home function because of electricity. Imagine living without it! Our ancestors lived without electricity, and many people around the world still live this way. How would your life be different without electricity? Look up the word "<u>renewable</u>" in the dictionary. There are two types of <u>energy</u>, depending on its source: renewable energy and <u>non-renewable</u> energy. Renewable energy, or clean energy, is energy that comes from a never-ending source and it reproduces quickly. Examples of renewable energy include: solar energy, <u>eolic energy</u> (from the wind), <u>hydraulic energy</u> (from water), <u>geothermal energy</u> (heat from inside the earth),and <u>tidal energy</u> (from the ebb and flow of the sea). Non-renewable energy or <u>conventional</u> (common) energy, is energy that comes from a limited source, that could be used up. This is why we must think creatively about how we use energy. Examples of non-renewable energy sources include: <u>fossil fuels</u> (like coal, petroleum, and natural gas) and <u>nuclear fuels</u> (uranium and plutonium; elements found underground).

Write - Draw

Give an example of an item that is powered by each type of energy:

Environment

Solar energy: _____

Eolic energy: _____

Hydraulic energy: _____

Geothermal energy: _____

Tidal energy: _____

Fossil fuel: _____

Nuclear fuel: _____

Understand

People have discovered and created different forms of energy from resources in our surrounding environment. We have renewable energy, which does less harm to our natural environment than non-renewable energy. As the <u>administrators</u> (overseers, stewards) of our natural environment, we should seek creative ways to make changes in our use of natural resources, continue to create products that improve our quality of life, and, all the time, take care of our world.

Activity - Build a windmill - Eolic energy.

Materials - 8 x 8 inch paper, 1 small wooden stick, scissors, and a brass brad or pin. Instructions:

- Fold the square paper in half.
- Fold the paper again in half. Open the paper.
- Mark the <u>diagonal</u> lines.
- Cut along the diagonal markings; be careful not to cut all the way to the center
- Fold each point toward the center, secure them with the brad as you pin them onto the wooden stick... let it blow!

Reflect

How can I use renewable energy in my everyday life?

**Willpower**

I recognize and am responsible in using the energy in the world around me.

The World Around Me

Goal To learn how to protect and improve my natural environment

Pathways

Read

Planet Earth is a gift to us. Its beautiful sceneries, valuable resources, different climates and all the creatures living in it exist for us to enjoy and appreciate. It provides richly for our daily needs. Like any other gift, it requires maintenance (care, attention), even more so because it sustains our lives. If we are not respectful of our environment, tending to its needs, and generous in sharing what it yields, we will lose nature's beauty as we know it, and will endanger our own survival.

Our daily actions affect the planet and its natural resources in a positive or negative way and determine the health of our planet. Take a moment to consider how your actions affect your environment.

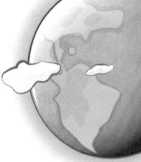

Understand

Is the following helpful or harmful? Draw a happy face if the action helps the environment, or a sad face if it harms the environment.

- Throw garbage in its proper place.
- Plant a tree with my family.
- Leave the lights on at home.
- Turn the television off when I am not using it.
- Choose products that can be reused or recycled.
- Use rechargeable batteries.
- Let the water run while I brush my teeth.

Write - Draw

Think of one other positive action that you can take to benefit the environment. Draw a picture of the action and write two sentences to explain how it helps the environment.

_____

_____

_____

_____

_____

_____

_____

_____

Apply - make a difference, plant tomatoes!

- Place a tomato seed between two pieces of cotton.
- Wet the cotton with water.
- Place it inside a small cup.
- Repeat the process with a bean.
- Place one cup in the sun and the other in the shade.
- Each day, observe what happens in each cup.

Reflect

How does planting seeds make a difference to the environment? What are some actions you do that could be hurting the environment? How can you change them? Make two commitments/goals that will help your take better care of the Earth.

1. _____

2. _____

Willpower

I am committed to protecting and improving my environment to the best of my ability.

NOTES

ECONOMICS

Discover how to handle money successfully by understanding the difference between wealth, value, and true success. As a result, you will learn how to increase the resources that are available to you.

Your ability to create wealth with the resources available to you gives you the opportunity to share yourself with others and impact their well-being, which is important for experiencing peace and happiness. That is how you design your future, or leave your fingerprint on humanity.

Prized Possessions

Goal   To understand what is truly important in my life

Pathways

Activity - "Let's go!"

Imagine you will be taking a journey to a deserted island. You will stay on the island for three months. The only food available on the island is fish and coconuts. Decide what you will take with you on your trip. What can't you live without? Draw or write down the items in your suitcase.

Comment

Do you consider the things you chose as your most <u>prized</u> <u>possessions</u>? Why?

What is missing in your suitcase to have an unforgettable trip?

What or who is important to you that cannot be placed in a suitcase?

Are these people or things more important than what goes into your suitcase?

Understand

There are material items that we value very much (things like toys, game consoles, bikes, etc.). We even think we cannot live without them. Did you think about the people in your life when you made the list above? We all enjoy the phone we use, the clothes we wear, the car our family drives, the house we live in and the money we spend, but these <u>external</u> material things can be taken away from us at any time. And then what? We will discover that the really important things; the things we truly cannot live without are the people we interact with and love.

The true wealth of every nation is in its people. When
a country or a city experiences a <u>disaster</u>, people may not
have <u>access</u> to their cars, possessions, or homes. Very often, the
only thing left are other people around them who <u>extend</u> their hands
and their care, who share what they have and help to rebuild what was lost.

On a <u>deserted</u> island we would discover that our true treasures are not the
material items we tend to value so much, but the people we have in our lives.

Write

Who are the important people in your life?

Think of three people (or relationships) you have that are of great value to you.

Write each one on the line and explain why each one is valuable to you.

1. _____: _____

   _____

   _____: _____

   _____

2. _____: _____

   _____

Reflect

When I value something or someone, how do I demonstrate that?

Do I tell the people who are important to me that I value them? How?

What are some ways to show others (through actions) that I hold them dear?

What is a valuable moment or experience you shared with your family?

What do I value about myself?

How do I demonstrate to friends and family that I value myself?

The relationships I have with people are the most important possessions I have.

World's #1 Resource: People

Goal

Pathways

To understand the value of others

Observe

At first glance you will see two drawings that seem to be <u>identical</u>, but after looking carefully you will be able to find seven differences between the drawings. Can you find them?

Comment

Was it difficult to find the differences?

Did you enjoy finding the differences and similarities?

Think about the people in your life—their differences and similarities.

What would life be like if we were all the same in every possible way?

What are some benefits of being different and unique?

See if you can list at least 3 benefits.

1. _____

2. _____

3. _____

Understand

People are the most important aspect of our life. The better we understand this, the greater our relationships can become, because we learn to value each and every one for who they are. Each person is different physically, mentally, emotionally, and

70

spiritually. Even identical twins are very different from each other and hold their own identities. How we are designed makes us special and unique. Our different gifts and talents give us the opportunity to share ourselves in our own unique way with others around us. These are the qualities that make us who we are. It is amazing how each person can dream, invent, and create things in special ways that positively impact their surrounding world.

Create

What do you imagine the circle could be?
Use your creativity to use or decorate it.

Comment

Compare your circle design with those of your classmates. Did anyone do the same thing with the circle?

What are your thoughts on the different circle art works your class produced?

Why does your design look different from your classmates' designs? Did any of the other designs come close to what you created?

Do you prefer some circle art more than others? Why?

If each person's circle was put on display in your classroom, would they be interesting to look at if all of them were exactly the same?

Reflect

Name at least two ways in which you are creative, unique and special.

How do these characteristics impact the people around you?

Is it hard to be <u>original</u>? Why?

Do you fear being unique and different? Why?

Willpower

Everyone is <u>authentic</u> and unique, and that
makes life interesting.

Structuring Time

Goal

To learn to <u>maximize</u> my time

Pathways

Draw

<u>Mingle</u>! Find different students who fit each statement and write their names on the lines.

1. _____ wakes up at 6:00 am.
2. _____ wakes up earlier than 6:00 am.
3. _____ wakes up later than 6:00 am.
4. _____ eats dinner at 5:00 pm.
5. _____ eats dinner at 6:00 pm.
6. _____ goes to bed before 8:00 pm.
7. _____ goes to bed after 9:00 pm.
8. _____ does their homework before dinner.
9. _____ does their homework after dinner.
10. _____ helps with chores after school.

Comment

Do you eat your meals at the same time each day?

Do you wake up and go to bed at the same time each day?

Do you have a <u>scheduled</u> time each day to do your homework?

To exercise? To play with friends? To help with chores?

What things do you spend most of your day doing?

Is it important to have a schedule for all of your activities? Why?

Understand

Time is a valuable non-renewable resource. As the hours, minutes, and seconds pass, we can never again regain them. All people, <u>regardless</u> of social class, <u>background</u>, or <u>origin</u>, count on the same measure of time. However, there is a great difference between what people accomplish within the same amount of time. Consistently scheduling your time and activities will help you <u>manage</u> your time in the best way possible. As you do, you will discover that you can get far more done than you thought! Making daily, weekly, monthly and yearly plans and schedules about the goals you want to achieve helps you <u>define</u> how and what needs to happen, and when it would be best to do so. It also breaks down what might seem to be <u>unreachable</u> goals into smaller steps that can be accomplished. Writing these goals and steps down will cause you to focus, give you clarity, save you time and put your <u>tasks</u> in order, from the most important to the least important. If you develop this habit and follow this <u>pattern</u>, you will have time to create, work, play, and rest.

Activity

Simon and Allen go to school until 2:00 pm. After school, they participate in sports until 3:30 pm. They also have to do chores and do their homework, all before dinner at 6:30 pm.

Simon's Chores:
- Sweep the kitchen floor.
- Take out the trash.
- Walk the dog.

Allen's Chores:
- Water the flowers.
- Fold your clothes.
- Empty the dishwasher.

Help Simon and Allen organize their schedules so they can accomplish their chores in time.

Simon	
Time	Activity

Allen	
Time	Activity

Reflect

Make a weekly schedule for yourself of all the daily activities you take part in.

I organize my time, <u>prioritize</u> my activities, and <u>evaluate</u> the results on a daily basis.

 Goal To learn to see all situations from a positive and creative point of view

Pathways

 Read

"The Stone" - a poem by Antonio Pereira Apon, translated by Josien Knigge

The distracted stumbled over it.

The brute used it as a projectile.

The entrepreneur built with it.

The tired farmhand made it a seat.

For the child it was a toy.

Drummond poeticized about it.

David killed Goliath with it.

The artist created a beautiful sculpture from it.

In all of these cases, the difference was not the stone but the man.

This poem shows that every stone or obstacle in your path can be used in many different ways, and can even help you achieve greatness by accomplishing tasks set before you. However, its purpose depends on you and how you decide to use it for your benefit. Think of what you would use the stone for and write about it.

_____

_____

_____

_____

_____

 Comment

Share your ideas with your classmates.

What can we learn from the poem, "The Stone"?

Understand

Every day we will find obstacles in our way. These <u>hurdles</u> provide <u>opportunities</u> to create and invent new things or learn more about ourselves and our environment. However, our success in overcoming these hurdles is determined by our attitude and creativity. If we practice looking at hurdles and things that frustrate us from a different <u>viewpoint</u>, they just might turn out to be a key to our success and future. Our point of view can and will change the outcome of a situation!

Create

Pretend to be inventors in the "Land of the Alternate Inventions"

- Form groups of 3 people.
- Imagine you live in a land of inventors; everyone invents something, and everything that is invented is accepted by everyone else.
- Each group chooses an object and invents new ways to use it.
- The group that gives the greatest varieties of uses to the chosen object, wins.
- The object your group chose was:

_____

The new uses that were given to this object are:

_____

_____

Reflect

How do I react in my daily life when I face an obstacle?

Do I look at these difficult situations in a positive way?

Do I try to use all of life's events in a positive manner? How?

If not, how can I change that?

Willpower

I take advantage of every obstacle and challenge because I know it is an opportunity to learn and grow.

Goal   To learn that there are no limits to accomplishing my dreams

Pathways

Read

One day, a striped caterpillar was walking toward the sun. On the way, a grasshopper asked him: "Where are you headed?" Without stopping, the caterpillar answered, "I had a dream last night. I dreamed that from the top of the great mountain, I looked down at the <u>entire</u> valley. I liked what I saw in the dream and I decided to fulfill my dream." The grasshopper said, "You must be crazy! How are you going to make it up there? You, a simple caterpillar? Even a small puddle or a tree trunk could be an <u>impassable</u> <u>barrier</u> to you." But the caterpillar kept moving and was determined not to let the grasshopper discourage him. The spider, the mole, and the frog all told him it was impossible. But nothing stopped the caterpillar.

A little tired, the caterpillar decided to rest for a while. "I will accomplish my dream, but I must first stop to rest," was the last thing the caterpillar said before he laid down to sleep. As time went on, the animals realized that the caterpillar was nowhere to be found. They feared something terrible had happened to him on his journey. Then one morning, when the sun shone bright in the sky, the animals received news of something unusual happening just outside of town.

They all rushed to the large <u>milkweed</u> bush just outside the village limits, and were amazed at what they saw. There hung a hard green shell, which began to break. With great <u>astonishment</u>, they saw eyes and <u>antennae</u> <u>emerge</u> that couldn't possibly belong to a caterpillar. Little by little, the beautiful wings of a butterfly fluttered out from its shell. Indeed, the caterpillar had transformed into a strong <u>monarch butterfly</u> and now would be able to accomplish his dream of flying to the top of the mountain!

Comment

What was the caterpillar's dream?

Did the caterpillar <u>encounter</u> obstacles? What were they?

What did the other animals think of the caterpillar's dream?

Do you have a dream that you haven't shared with anyone?

 Understand

Each of us has been given a unique mind that allows us to dream, and we also have the drive to accomplish these dreams. Nothing and no one can stop us from accomplishing our dreams if we truly believe we can achieve them. Our confidence in ourselves must be greater than the negative advice of the people around us or the barriers in life that will try to stop us. We just need to use our creativity and determination until we accomplish our goal.

 Activity

Think about your dreams and goals while you complete the following sentences.

My dream is _____

What can stop me from living my dream is _____

I am not limited to _____

I have _____

I can accomplish _____

I will <u>achieve</u> _____

"<u>Persevere</u>" means _____

Reflect

Take a moment to think about your dreams. What is your purpose in life?

How do you plan on accomplishing your dreams?

Name three things you will need in order to achieve your dreams? Why?

Willpower

I know that I am able and capable of accomplishing my dreams.

Glossary

Access: freedom to make use of something (#69)

Accompany: go with (#47)

Accomplish: bring to completion (#57)

Achieve: to carry out with success (#77)

Adequate: enough to meet the need (#55)

Administrators: people in a management role (#63)

Adolescence: stage of human development in ages 10-19 (#18)

Adopted: taken in as part of a family (#40)

Affection: feelings of love or devotion (#28)

Affects: produces a change in; impact felt (#16) (#26)

Affirmative: encouraging; positive (#41)

Amazed: great wonder or surprise (#36)

Antennae: a pair of slender, moveable organs on the heads of insects (#76)

Anxious: fearful; strong pressure (#48)

Appearance: the way something or someone looks (#57)

Appears: looks like (#34)

Ashamed: feeling of guilt or embarrassment (#47)

Assign: to delegate a task (#56)

Astonishment: great surprise; wonder and amazement (#76)

Attention: applying your thoughts to something or someone (#21)

Attentively: act of focusing your thoughts on (#42)

Attitude: a feeling or emotion towards something (#22)

Authentic: being exactly as it appears (#71)

Background: place time and setting when something occurs (#72)

Balanced: having different parts properly arranged (#27)

Bandanna: a large colorful handkerchief (#14)

Barrier: something that blocks passage (#76)

Behavior: the manner of conducting oneself (#16)

Bond: a coming together or binding (#13)

Boundaries: limits to how far something can go (#20)

Brute: of animal quality or harsh (#74)

Capable: showing general ability (#46)

Carved: cut with care and precision (#22)

Category: a basic division or grouping of things (#56)

Caterpillar: the worm-like insect that transforms to a butterfly or moth (#54)

Challenges: difficult tasks or problems (#32)

Characteristics: special qualities or appearances in an individual (#18)

Circumstances: events that affect a situation (#36)

Climates: the average weather conditions of a place (#64)

Common: used frequently; not unusual (#12)

Compare: to examine for similarity or differences (#13)

Compassion: pity for and a desire to help someone (#45)

Complex: not easy to understand (#28) (#55)

Compliments: best wishes of respect and admiration (#28)

Condition: to change the habits of usually by training (#34)

Confident: certain about your ability to do things well (#21)

Confidentiality: to keep other people's information secret (#11)

Conflicts: extended struggles (#49)

Consequences: the effects following bad decisions (#27)

Consider: to think about carefully (#14)

Considerate: thoughtful of the rights and feelings of others (#42)

Consistent: always the same (#57)

Content: pleased and satisfied; not needing more (#30)

Conventional: following the usual or accepted way of doing things (#62)

Conversation: a talk between two or more people (#27)

Corresponding: having qualities in common (#50)

Courage: strength of heart to carry on even in danger (#21)

Courteous: showing consideration and good manners (#17)

Create: is to produce something from nothing. It is to speak invisible things like thoughts, ideas and imaginations into existence. Words frame the thoughts that create your reality. Life is the culmination of your words (#4)

Criticize: to find fault with (#42)

Cultures: the habits, beliefs and traditions of a particular people (#45)

Current: the directional flow of water (#37)

Damaging: causing harm or loss to (#27)

Decorate: to make more attractive (#29)

Dedication: an act of setting apart for a special purpose (#41)

Define: to explain the meaning of (#73)

Deflate: take air out of (#34)

Dependable: capable of being trusted (#50)

Descriptions: written or spoken statements about something (#44)

Deserted: left without intending to return (#69)

Design: to think up and plan out in the mind (#28)

Destiny: what happens to someone or something in the future (#36)

Detailed: including many small items or parts (#29)

Determination: firm or fixed intention (#36)

Determine: to come to a decision (#64)

Development: the state of or result of maturing and changing (#55)

Devoted: completely loyal (#40)

Diagonal: running from one corner to the opposite corner (#63)

Disaster: something that happens suddenly and causes suffering or loss (#69)

Disrupt: to interrupt the normal course of (#43

Distinct: easy to notice or understand (#45)

Distracted: have attention drawn to something else (#43)

Distribute: to divide among many (#15)

Donate: to make a gift of (#46)

Drawn: to take out of (#62)

Drummond: a Scottish writer and clergyman (#74)

Effective: able to produce a desired result (#56)

Efficient: bringing about a desired result with little waste (#56)

Emerge: to come out or into view (#76)

Emotions: strong feelings along with physical reactions (#28)

Empathy: the understanding and sharing of the emotions of another person (#45)

Encounter: to meet or come face to face (#77)

Encourage: to give help or support to (#28)

Encouraging: giving hope or confidence to (#16)

Endanger: to expose to harm (#55)

Endured: put up with (#51)

Energy: ability to be active; strong action or effort (#62)

Enthusiasm: strong feeling in favor of something (#28)

Entire: complete in all parts (#76)

Entrepreneur: an individual who creates a new business (#74)

Environment: a person's physical surroundings (#28)

Eolic Energy: power created by the wind (#62)

Evaluate: to judge the value or condition of (#73)

Explore: to go into for purposes of discovery or adventure (#35)

Extend: to make longer or larger (#69)

Extensive: including or affecting many things (#55)

Extent: the distance or range that is covered (#55)

External: situated on or relating to the outside (#68)

Family: is a household consisting of parents and children living together. Because of life circumstances sometimes there are different formations of family units. Family forms culture and determines values. It should be a safe place. (#4)

Faithful: firm in devotion or support (#40)

Farmhand: a farm worker (#74)

Fixed Mindset: a mental attitude that is not willing to change (#32)

Flexible: easy to bend (#23)

Food chain: living things depending on each other for food (#54)

Forgiving: ready or willing to excuse an error or offense (#28)

Fossil fuels: a fuel formed in the earth from plant or animal remains (#62)

Fuel: substance that can be burned to produce power (#62)

Gain: an increase in amount (#50)

Generate: to cause to come into being (#62)

Generous: freely giving or sharing (#30)

Gentle: soft and delicate (#42)

Geothermal Energy: energy that uses heat from inside the earth (#62)

Gnawing: biting or chewing on with the teeth (#51)

Grit: strength of mind or spirit (#36)

Growth Mindset: a person's belief in the their own ability to learn and develop skills (#32)

Habit: usual way of behaving (#57)

Habitats: places where plants or animals naturally live and grow (#55)

Harsh: severe or cruel; not kind (#16)

Humble: not proud or arrogant (#22)

Humored: made to laugh (#51)

Hunch: a strong feeling concerning a future event or result (#21)

Hurdles: barriers or obstacles (#75)

Hydraulic Energy: energy that is operated or brought about by means of water (#62)

Identical: being exactly alike or equal (#70)

Imaginative: showing an ability to think of new and interesting ideas (#35)

Impact: a strong effect (#31)

Impassable: impossible to pass, cross or travel (#76)

Implies: suggests rather than says plainly (#41)

Improve: to make or become better (#27)

Incredible: too improbable to be believed (#36)

Infancy: a beginning or early period of existence (#18)

Inflate: to expand or increase with air (#34)

Influence: to affect in an indirect usually important way (#26)

Inspirational: something that is moving or felt with emotion (#61)

Instructions: outline of how something is to be done (#13)

Insult: an act or statement showing disrespect (#42)

Interacting: talking or doing things with other people (#61)

Internal: being within something; within the body (#21)

Invention: something that is created or produced for the first time (#28)

Inventor: a person who creates or produces new things (#59)

Irritated: made sensitive or sore (#49)

Items: things in a list or series (#58)

Judge: to form an opinion after careful consideration (#42)

Knit: to make clothes (#28)

Lack: to need or be without something (#21)

Leadership: is to lead, administrate, manage, or to go before. The action of leading people or an organization. It is the ability to influence others through words and deeds. (#4)

Lend: to give usually for a time (#46)

Life cycle: a series of stages someone or something passes through during their lifetime (#18)

Limits: boundary lines (#21)

Love: It is a personal decision to give the best you have for the wellbeing of another, independent of merit and without expecting anything in return. True love is unconditional (#4)

Loyal: showing true and constant support (#41)

Magnificent: very beautiful or impressive (#36)

Manage: to look after and make decisions about (#73)

Mature: fully grown or developed (#18)

Maximize: to make the most of (#72)

Maze: a confusing arrangement of paths or passages (#46)

Meerkats: an African mongoose; small burroughing animal (#15)

Menu: the dishes available for or served at a meal (#27)

Milkweed: a plant with milky juice and clusters for flowers (#76)

Mindful: keep in thoughts; aware (#60)

Mingle: to move among others within a group (#72)

Mini Workshop: a short session to teach others something (#33)

Mistreat: abuse; be mean to (#60)

Moderator: the chairman of a discussion group (#49)

Modest: descent in thought, conduct and dress; something smaller than others (#22)

Mold: to work and press into shape (#22)

Monarch Butterfly: a large orange and black American butterfly (#76)

Morals: principles of right and wrong in behavior (#22)

Non-renewable: not capable of being replaced (#62)

Nuclear fuels: fuel that provides nuclear energy as in power stations (#62)

Obstacle: something that stands in the way or opposes (#74)

Odds: conditions that make something difficult (#36)

Opportunities: chances for greater success (#75)

Optimistic: expecting good things to happen (#32)

Organizational: ability to put things in neat and structured arrangement (#57)

Origin: the point at which something begins (#72)

Original: not copied from anything else; the first (#71)

Participant: a person who takes part in something (#33)

Pattern: a model or guide for making something (#73)

Persevere: to keep trying to do something in spite of difficulties (#77)

Persistence: refusing to give up; continuing to do something (#36)

Personalities: human beings' unique qualities (#45)

Phases: steps or parts in a series of events (#18)

Phrase: a group of two or more words that express a single idea (#50)

Planet: any large heavenly body that orbits a star (#64)

Pleasant: having pleasing manners, behavior or appearance (#30)

Poeticized: to give a poetic quality to (#74)

Polite: showing courtesy or good manners (#21)

Possessions: things that are held by someone as property (#68)

Predators: animals that live mostly by killing and eating other animals (#36)

Prefer: to like better than another (#57)

Pressure: the need to get things done (#21)

Prioritize: to put in order based on importance (#73)

Prized: highly valued (#68)

Produce: is to generate, to make, to yield or give results. Small things can produce great results. Inside every seed is the image of a plant, but not just one plant, acres of plants or trees. (#4)

Productive: having the power to yield in large amounts (#57)

Profitable: producing a benefit or monetary gain (#59)

Projectile: something thrown or shot especially from a weapon (#74)

Promise: a statement by a person about their future actions (#50)

Purposefully: having a clear intention or aim (#19)

Purpose: is the reason for which something is done or created or for which something exists, it gives direction and meaning. When purpose is known every action can be judged as to whether it is on purpose or off purpose. Living on purpose saves time and hastens success. Purpose is why we have destiny. Purpose gives intention and avoids abuse and misuse. (#4)

Raging: extreme force (#36)

Rapids: part of the river where the current is fast (#36)

Rechargeable: able to regain energy (#64)

Recognize: to know and remember upon seeing (#22)

Recycling: adapting to a new use (#58)

Referee: a person who makes sure players follow the rules of a game or sport (#49)

Reflection: an image as if by a mirror (#57)

Reflect: show image like in a mirror (#57)

Regardless: in spite of something that might be a problem (#72)

Relate: to have a relationship or to connect (#37)

Relationships: the state of being related or connected (#28)

Reliable: fit to be trusted (#41)

Renewable: capable of being replaced (#62)

Represent: to act for or in place of (#44)

Re-purpose: to give a new purpose or use to (#58)

Requires: something that is necessary to succeed (#64)

Respect: high or special regard (#20)

Review: to look at or study again (#28)

Role: the job done by a member of a team or family (#13)

Rooting: encouraging a contestant or team; cheering (#37)

Routine: a usual way and order of doing something (#35)

Satisfaction: content; the condition of being well pleased (#15)

Sceneries: pleasant outdoor scenes or views (#64)

Scheduled: set on a timetable; put on the calendar (#72)

Sculpted: carved or molded into a particular shape (#22)

Sensitivity: taking care to do what is best for another; careful to not hurt others (#47)

Signature: the name of a person written by that person (#43)

Similar: having qualities in common (#21)

Sincere: having or showing honesty (#41)

Skills: developed or acquired abilities (#14)

Sorry: feeling sorrow or regret (#30)

Stage: a specific time period in the development of something (#18)

Statement: something stated or written in a formal way (#33)

Strained: not easy or natural (#35)

Strategy: a careful plan or method (#48)

Stung: (sting) sharp quick prick, bite or pain caused by an object, plants, insect or other anima (#26)

Styles: qualities that are felt to be very respectable or fashionable (#45)

Succeed: to turn out well; to achieve a desired result (#14)

Surroundings: the conditions or things around an individual; environment (#34)

Survive: to remain alive; to continue to exist (#36)

Talent: unusual natural ability (#33)

Tasks: pieces of work that have been assigned (#73)

Tidal Energy: a hydro-power that transforms the movement of tides into electricity (#62)

Transformed: changed completely into something new (#59)

Trial: hardship or problem (#51)

Trustworthy: worthy of confidence (#41)

Tugged: pulled hard (#51)

Uncomfortable: feeling discomfort or uneasiness (#47)

Unique: being the only one of its kind (#36)

Unreachable: impossible to get to or get out (#73)

Untangle: to remove a tangle from; to straighten out (#48)

Vaccinations: preparations that are given usually by injections to protect against a certain disease (#61)

Value: worth, usefulness or importance (#19)

Viewpoint: a way of looking or thinking about something (#75)

Volunteer: a person who does something by free choice without expecting to be paid (#28)

Wear: the damage done to something by its use (#34)

Well-being: state of being happy and healthy (#26)

Work: is activity involving mental or physical effort done in order to achieve a purpose, it is to serve. It is a way to share your unique strengths, abilities, knowledge and ideas with those around you, generally creating satisfaction within you. (#4)

Yanks: pulls suddenly or forcefully (#48)

NOTES

Need Help?

 Bullying/Fear
Remedy Live
Text: Remedy to 494949

 General Assistance
211.org
Phone: 211

 Runaway Youth
Boystown
Phone: 800-448-3000

 Eating Disorders
Timberline Knolls
Phone: 855-278-7960

 HOPE Line
Phone or text: 919-231-4525
Call: 1-877-2325-4525

 Violence
Family Violence Prevention Center
Phone: 210-733-8810

 Suicide, Depression, or Self-harm
Children of the Night
Phone: 800-551-1300

 Child Sexual Abuse
Childhelp National Child Abuse Hotline
Phone: 800-422-4453

HOPE★RISING
SOCIAL EMOTIONAL LEARNING